6 KEYS OF SPIRITUAL TRANSFORMATION

DR. DAVID CARUTH

WESTBOW°
PRESS
A DIVISION OF THOMAS NELSON
& ZONDERVAN

Scripture quotations, unless otherwise indicated, are from the King James Version (KJV) of the Holy Bible.

The 6 Keys of Spiritual Transformation cover was designed by David Caruth and imaged by Tolu Onasanya. Requests for permission to use cover design can be addressed to God's Perfect Timing Ministries, P.O. Box 70080, Washington, DC 20024.

The 6 Keys of Spiritual Transformation illustration was designed by David Caruth, and imaged by Tolu Onasanya. Requests for permission to use illustration can be addressed to God's Perfect Timing Ministries, P.O. Box 70080, Washington, DC 20024.

The Law of Spiritual Transformation illustration was designed by David Caruth, and imaged by Tolu Onasanya. Requests for permission to use illustration can be addressed to God's Perfect Timing Ministries, P.O. Box 70080, Washington, DC 20024.

WestBow Press books may be ordered through booksellers or by contacting:

WestBow Press
A Division of Thomas Nelson & Zondervan
1663 Liberty Drive
Bloomington, IN 47403
www.westbowpress.com
1 (866) 928-1240

Because of the dynamic nature of the Internet, any web addresses or links contained in this book may have changed since publication and may no longer be valid. The views expressed in this work are solely those of the author and do not necessarily reflect the views of the publisher, and the publisher hereby disclaims any responsibility for them.

Soft cover and e-book copies of this book may be ordered directly from the author at www.davidcaruth.com

ISBN: 978-1-4908-3166-4 (sc)
ISBN: 978-1-4908-3167-1 (e)

Library of Congress Control Number: 2014905806

Printed in the United States of America.

WestBow Press rev. date: 4/14/2014

For Adrian, Maya, Evie and Little Dave.

"Education is the most powerful weapon
you can use to change the world."

Nelson Mandela

CONTENTS

CHAPTER ONE

THE LAW OF SPIRITUAL TRANSFORMATION

"And be not conformed to this world: but be ye transformed by the renewing of your mind, that ye may prove what is that good, and acceptable, and perfect will of God." Romans 12:2

For years, pastors, teachers, ministers, and scholars worked diligently to find ways to help people transform their thinking and ultimately change their lives. I count myself among them. To bring about change in a global society, we need a deeper understanding of Spiritual Transformation, and new models for teaching and learning.

This book brings forth an enhanced level of spiritual understanding that ordinary people can use to transform their thinking, and ultimately renew their minds. I introduce original thought that emerged from my doctoral research on transformative learning. (Caruth,

D. 2000) My research findings expanded upon research by Jack Mezirow (1991).

I also drew upon wisdom gained from my understanding of scripture, diversity, poverty, and experiential knowledge in all of their complexities. I share knowledge gained from higher education, having read hundreds of books, biblical studies with pastors and ministers, and having attended church and ministerial conferences, where Apostles, Bishops, Pastors and Ministers enhanced my understanding.

The Spiritual Transformation I discuss in this book is not an emotional experience that can be easily described and understood. It is a scripture-based process of healing that transforms the psycho-cultural assumptions that distort the way we see ourselves. I introduce 6 Keys that illuminate a new process of learning, and will enhance your understanding of the Law of Spiritual Transformation.

After more than 10 years of utilizing and evaluating the effectiveness of this scripture-based model of transformational learning, I noticed that it worked in multiple settings: my personal relationships, the work environment, and especially when I used it to provide spiritual guidance so people can better navigate difficult challenges in their lives. That was the rewarding part.

The more challenging part was putting pen to paper and revealing a new level of understanding to the scrutiny of my wife Debra (an Ordained Minister in her own right), my family, and the discerning minds of my colleagues in the faith community. I am especially grateful Debra read multiple rough drafts of this book, and made suggestions that improved my work.

Shortly after I started writing this book, I realized that I would have to share parts of my spiritual journey to becoming a Teacher, in the Biblical sense. Sharing my spiritual journey, or personal testimony of the glory and power of God, has enabled me to fulfill the call on my life to teach people how to transform their thinking, renew their minds, and stand on their faith in God.

I was led by the Spirit and visited numerous churches. I bore witness to how pastors and ministers used their spiritual gifts to encourage people to change their behaviors. Most of them used Wisdom, Faith, and Exhortation to teach people how to transform their thinking. The 6 Keys of Spiritual Transformation will infuse your preaching and teaching with spiritual understanding, and will enhance your efforts to bring about the change people seek to inherit the Kingdom of God, and live more abundant lives.

While on this spiritual journey, during the course of normal conversations, I listened. People I encountered spoke about challenges they faced, including various forms of abuse, marital strife, alcohol and drug use, poor health, or financial issues caused by poverty, job loss or divorce. They expressed frustration with their inability to bring about permanent change in their lives. Their lack of success in finding permanent solutions to their problems caused many of them to lose faith in God, the power of prayer, the Holy Scripture, and often led them down paths towards spiritual brokenness, unhealthy relationships, and into poverty.

To help people break free from what they described as debilitating challenges in their lives, I used the spiritual gifts deposited in me by the Holy Spirit to determine when, and how to use the 6 Keys to speak into their lives. Using this scripture-based model of teaching enabled me to communicate spiritual truths revealed by my obedience to teach the word of God.

The 6 Keys of Spiritual Transformation, together with a deeper understanding of Romans 12:2, has led to a model of learning and teaching techniques that will bridge gaps in your understanding of diverse segments of society. Your attention to details in each of the 6 Keys will enable you to receive spiritually empowered teaching. This enhanced level of spiritual understanding will help people from diverse racial/ethnic groups and cultural backgrounds transform their thinking, change their actions, and develop new worldviews of what is possible.

SPIRITUAL GIFTS

"Now concerning spiritual gifts, brethren, I would not have you ignorant." 1 Corinthians 12:1

My understanding of Spiritual Gifts is ground in the Holy Scripture. 1 Corinthians 12:4 teaches us, *"there are diversities of gifts, but the same Spirit."* Some gifts are mentioned by name including: the Word of Wisdom, Word of Knowledge, Discerning of Spirits (1 Corinthians 12:8-10), and Exhortation (Romans 12:8). There are many other spiritual gifts, and all are important blessings from God.

The scripture also provides guidance on the Spiritual Gifts appointed to the church. 1 Corinthians 12:28-29 teaches us, *"And God hath set some in the church, first apostles, secondarily prophets, thirdly teachers, after that, miracles, then gifts of healing, helps, governments, diversities of tongues. Are all apostles? are all prophets? are all teachers? are all workers of miracles?"* If we understand the power and responsibilities the Holy Scripture attaches to spiritual gifts, we know that we have to work together, as one body of Christ, if we expect to help people transform their lives and live in the grace of God.

Given the diversity of gifts, it is also important to understand that people can expect to have different measures of their particular gifts. Romans 12: 6-7 teaches us that, *"Having then gifts differing according to the grace that is given to us, whether prophecy, let us prophecy according to the proportion of faith; Or ministry, let us wait on ministering: or he that teacheth, on teaching."* It has been a blessing for me to learn about spiritual gifts from men and women of faith who were willing to teach me in person or at ministerial conferences. I also read the Holy Bible, and studied resources provided by other ministries.

My focus here is on the spiritual gift of Teaching. I am not talking about a person who teaches by virtue of a natural ability to teach, but someone who is called by God to teach by supernatural ability. The teaching that I refer to is by divine endowment, and is designed to create a tension in the mind. The discussion that follows illustrates how I use some of the spiritual gifts the Holy Spirit deposited in me, to provide you with an enhanced understanding of spiritual transformation.

During the course of ordinary conversations with people, I found myself using the spiritual gift of Discernment to determine which stage of Spiritual Transformation their minds were in, and to hear from God if they could receive my speaking into their lives. For my purposes here, Discernment is the ability to see beyond our natural circumstances to determine the value of a person's life-changing event, past the mere perception of it; making detailed judgments about the event; and determining if an action taken had good or evil intentions.

Some of you may be asking yourselves, why I chose to use Discernment when there are other spiritual gifts like Knowledge or Wisdom available to help people change their thinking and ultimately transform their lives. On my spiritual journey, most pastors and ministers used Knowledge and Wisdom to help people change their lives. I use them myself. For my purposes here, Knowledge is the ability to speak wisdom about a given situation into another's life.

As the Apostle Paul revealed to us in 1 Corinthians 1:5, the highest form of knowledge is the Gospel of Jesus Christ. Wisdom, gained through knowledge, is a powerful and useful gift, and is sufficient all by itself to bring about change. However, people who use mature discernment can tell the difference between their human or fleshly understanding of difficult life challenges, their spiritual understanding of those challenges, and if evil spirits of the enemy were working to separate a persons' understanding of the word of God from their actions.

Still others might suggest the spiritual gifts of Exhortation or Healing are more prominently used gifts to counsel people and help them change their behaviors. They may be right. What I have learned is that men and women of God use Exhortation, or primarily a "speaking" gift, to motivate people to change their behavior by encouraging, challenging, comforting, or guiding them to change their actions so that they can reach their full potentials.

While those who use the gift of Healing, or primarily a "laying on of hand" gift, help people change their lives by using the power of Jesus Christ to cure illness and restore a persons' wellbeing including physical, emotional, mental, and spiritual self by touching, prayer, or speaking scripture-based healing into someone's life. People who use the gifts of Exhortation or Healing demonstrate the power of God by using their gifts at opportune times to communicate Biblical truths, and provide evidence of the glory and power of the word of God. Proverbs 4:22, teaches us that the word of God is life unto those that find them, and health to all their flesh.

From my perspective as a Teacher, I encourage men and women of God to use the spiritual gifts the Holy Spirit deposited into you. When Apostles, Bishops, Priests, Pastors, Teachers, and Ministers understand how to use the 6 Keys of Spiritual Transformation to unlock The Law of Spiritual Transformation, they will enhance their abilities to help believers in their congregations break habits that have kept them from experiencing the blessings of living more abundant and fulfilling lives.

CHAPTER TWO

LACK OF KNOWLEDGE

"My people are destroyed for lack of knowledge: because thou has rejected knowledge, I will also reject thee, that thou shalt be no priest to me: seeing thou has forgotten The Law of thy God, I will also forget thy children." Hosea 4:6

Understanding the knowledge behind the 6 Keys of Spiritual Transformation will enhance the way you teach, motivate, and help people transform their lives. When you look back at the training you received as priests, pastors, teachers, or ministers, you may notice how the knowledge you received helped people commit their lives to Christ. However, there may be gaps in your ability to help the most vulnerable among us change their behaviors enough to break bad or otherwise unhealthy habits. Unfortunately, many of us can trace our lack of knowledge all the way back to elementary school.

Some of us, the ones fortunate enough to have received some type of standardized education as children, had teachers who helped us learn how to read, write and do math. If we went to the right schools, our teachers had several years of formal teacher education training and cared about us as students. If we were privileged and blessed, they used their teaching skills to enrich our learning by planting seeds of knowledge into the fertile ground of our minds.

As we moved from elementary school to middle school, we were fortunate if our schools were adequately staffed with knowledgeable teachers, libraries with up-to-date books, computers, and science laboratories. We were blessed if we learned how to manage our personal behaviors, and our schools were free from violence associated with racism, gangs, drug-use, and bullying.

If we were fortunate enough to reach high school, it was a blessing if our teachers helped us develop leadership skills and taught us to think critically about what we learned in school. Some might even consider it a minor miracle if teachers taught us how to apply what we learned in the classroom, to real situations in our lives.

However, many of us were not so fortunate. Some of us were born into poverty. Instead of focusing on nurturing the seeds of knowledge teachers planted in our minds, the seeds struggled to take root. The Holy Scripture teaches us in Matthew 13:5-6, that those seeds were planted on rocky ground.

How many times were our minds not able to focus on what was being taught because we were in survival mode? Instead of learning what other children were being taught, our poverty-stricken minds drifted back and forth between the physical pain of hunger and lack of adequate shelter, feeling safe, or how to survive the psychological pain of prejudice.

To make matters worse, some of our parents and other family members joined prejudiced or uncaring teachers and planted negative seeds of doubt in our minds. Still other among us may have been born addicted to drugs, or with debilitating or infectious diseases right out of the womb.

What happens in the minds of poverty-stricken children who longed to have a roof over their heads, with soft warm beds and pillows to rest their heads on, and went to bed hungry instead? Or were unable to sleep the night before because their parents argued and fought all night long? What about the child whose parents lost the family home altogether because they lost their job, were addicted to drugs or gambling, and the homeless child spent the night wandering the streets searching for food and a safe place to sleep?

What happens to young, fertile minds raised in public housing projects, where one or both parents were abusive, in jail, or merely unemployed for extended periods of time and gave up looking for work? As men and women of faith, you have to ask yourselves if the learning you received as pastors and ministers in Bible schools, universities, or seminary prepared you to transform the minds of those children, especially after they made mistake after mistake trying to find their way on the road to adulthood.

After high school, some of you were fortunate enough to graduate, get good paying jobs, marry your high school sweethearts, have children, and raise your children in family units. Some of you may have gone on to college, and enriched our minds with higher education.

Still others among us may not have been so fortunate. For some of us, life got in the way. Some of us dropped out of school along the way to adulthood, engaged in risky activities and ended up pregnant, in jail, or worse. Others turned towards the ways of the world, embraced crime, sold drugs, and used what we learned on the street to make a living hustling people.

Some of us simply crossed paths with corrupt officials or people who were sworn, by duty of their jobs to serve and protect, but instead of protecting us, set us up to take the fall for crimes we did not commit. Other people we expected to protect us turned a blind eye when we were getting abused, and some actively participated in our abuse. How are we, as leaders, expected to help the less fortunate among us transform their lives, if their ability to trust has been destroyed?

In Hosea 4:6, the scripture makes it plan that God's people are "destroyed for lack of knowledge." To destroy something means to put an end to its existence by damaging, attacking, or annihilating it. I am certain that most, if not all of you can speak about attacks on your person that you have withstood while on your own spiritual journeys. But have you learned enough about the poor, disadvantaged, or underprivileged to help them gain enough knowledge to break the cycle of poverty and other afflictions?

Proverbs 1:7 teaches us that *"the fear of the Lord is the beginning of knowledge: but fools despise wisdom and instruction."* Let all men and women of God prepare your minds to receive instruction, increase your understanding, and prove that you have not rejected knowledge.

CHAPTER THREE

6 KEYS OF SPIRITUAL TRANSFORMATION

"Give instruction to a wise man, and he will be yet wiser: teach a just man, and he will increase in learning." Proverbs 9:9

I encourage those who wish to master spiritual transformation to undergo Transformational Leadership Training at God's Perfect Timing Ministries before you use the 6 Keys to speak into people's lives. However, if you grasp the essence of the teachings presented, I pray that you use God's speed helping people renew their minds and transform their lives.

When I looked back and reflected on my spiritual journey for the last 20 years, what I saw surprised me. The Holy Spirit revealed to me that my experiential knowledge, academic training, and empirical research, prepared me to be a Teacher, in the Biblical sense. I learned how to use the spiritual gifts the Holy Spirit deposited in me so that I could answer the call God placed on my life.

Significant parts of the first half of my spiritual journey have already been published in my first book, God's Perfect Timing: Breaking the Cycle of Poverty with Education and Faith. I wrote that book as a personal testimony to the glory and power of God. I wanted people to see that God could take a child out of poverty, who spent grades 1-6 in Special Education classes, and was subjected to multiple kinds of abuse, and transform his life.

At football practice, as a high school senior, a bolt of lighting ripped through the clear blue sky and ended my life, yet I survived. In Job 38:35, the Holy Scripture asks, *"Canst thou send lightnings, that they may go, and say unto thee, Here we are?"* Following the lightning strike, I experienced death 2 more times in the hospital, spent 4 days in a coma, lost my hearing, and still ended up with a Ph.D. In God's Perfect Timing, I revealed miracle after miracle in my life. This book; however, has a different purpose.

The knowledge presented in this little book took me a lifetime to learn. Some of the examples I use to illustrate my points may challenge your thinking. Nonetheless, they reveal how the 6 Keys will enhance your understanding, increase your knowledge, and change the way you help people transform their lives.

The 6 Keys of Spiritual Transformation, as described and illustrated below, are sequential. For instance, the first Key: Disorientation, always occurs first in the learning process and is followed by the second Key, Critical Reflection; the third Key, Perspective Transformation; the fourth Key, Social Action; the fifth Key, Spirituality; and finally, The 6th Key, Change in Worldview.

6 Keys of Spiritual Transformation Illustration

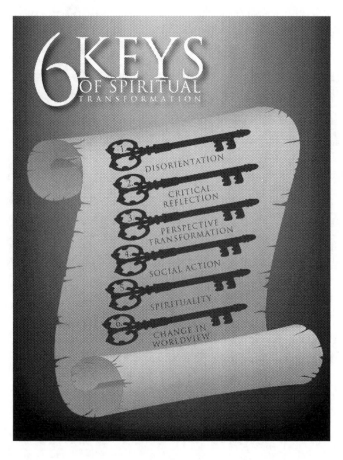

The knowledge contained within the 6 Keys will increase your understanding of Spiritual Transformation. Pay particular attention to the essential elements of all 6 Keys, their application, and use. It is likely that you will have to identify and use spiritual gifts the Holy Spirit has deposited in you, to help bring about the change members of your congregations desire. Use the 6 Keys to unlock The Law of Spiritual Transformation (Romans 12:2) and help people resist temptation, transform and renew their minds, and prove what is good and acceptable, and the perfect will of God.

THE FIRST KEY:
DISORIENTATION

The first Key of Spiritual Transformation is Disorientation, or a tension in the mind. Understanding that mature minds receive and process new learning differently from children is critical to your being able to help adults to transform their thinking.

A child's brain absorbs information through a process of learning commonly known as "knowledge formation." Teachers teach, and youthful brains receive information. This type of learning allows children to develop rote memory skills.

Children, who sit patiently in the classroom, listen to instruction or read quietly on their own, and repeat what they have learned at the request of the teacher, enable teachers to "grade" their ability to recall information that was being taught. Children that demonstrate mastery of this type of learning, receive high grades, praise and other types of rewards to encourage their continued adherence to this type of learning.

Unfortunately, in today's society, far too many of our youth are not able to sit quietly for long periods of time. Their ability to pay attention is compromised by constant stimulation of the Internet, cell phones, video games, and being placed in life or death situations. Far too many of our youth suffer from traumatic events in their lives, self-medicate or take prescription drugs, and struggle to learn on their way to adulthood. To make matters worse, they interact with adults who suffer from childhood traumatic stress, expose them to violence and crime, and doubt their ability to become productive members of society.

As a scholar and researcher in the area of Adult Learning, mature minds are more receptive to learning new knowledge during periods of Disorientation when eye-opening events occur in our lives. Job loss, divorce, or learning that you have an incurable illness, all create tension in the mind. However, not all Disorientations are negative. Getting married, reading a good book, winning the lotto, or going back to college for retraining also cause Disorientations.

Understanding that mature minds are receptive to learning new information during periods of Disorientation will better enable you to use different teaching styles to help people change their thinking. Some teachers use lecture, audio/video aids, Socratic dialog, written word, graphic aids, music, YouTube, photography, drama/movement, and other forms of communication to help people receive information during periods of Disorientation.

Unlike preachers in the past, you are no longer constrained by using auditory words of comfort, encouragement, or criticism to help people change. Howard Gardner (1993) suggests that you can use multiple theories of learning to help people learn new things. Some people learn best when they can see visual images of information that is being presented, while others learn better when their bodies are in motion. When you understand how to use Spiritual Transformation, the process of helping people change bad habits or break free from difficult life challenges like poverty, addiction, and even loss of faith becomes more manageable.

It is also important to understand that people experience multiple Disorientations normally throughout the day. For instance, when a father learns that his wife is about to give birth to their first child, we can expect his mind to be in a state of Disorientation.

On his way to the hospital, he may get pulled over for speeding. It might appear to the soon to be father, that the police officer unnecessarily delayed his effort to reach the hospital. His getting the speeding ticket may cause a second Disorientation.

When he gets to the hospital and wants to comfort his wife, his job may send him a text message stating that his boss needs the final draft of a presentation locked on his office computer. This may create a third Disorientation in his mind. Until his mind has time to work through all 6 stages of Spiritual Transformation, his ability to successfully resolve those particular challenges in his life may stall. If his mind stalls while experiencing multiple Disorientations, he may have long periods of mental anguish, get frustrated, and may imagine a reality far worse than what is actually happening in real life.

THE SECOND KEY:
CRITICAL REFLECTION

Learning how and why people go through Critical Reflection is essential to helping them learn new knowledge. Critical Reflection is a process of reflecting back on prior learning that empowers people to determine if knowledge learned in the past is relevant, or even worth hanging-on to, for future decision making purposes.

When people go through the critical reflection process, your communication must help them scrutinize assumptions, values, and norms that underscore periods of indecision and doubt. Your intercession must enable them to see and hear their reality with their minds. All too often, people make choices they later regret because they see reality with their eyes, hear it with their ears, and follow the voice of the enemy.

In the previous example, I discussed a first time father who experienced multiple Disorientations. However, life is more complex than what I provided in the scenario. How would you respond if the father lived in Detroit during the 2008 recession, and you had to minister to hundreds of people going through multiple disorientations?

Detroit's population declined from a peak of 1.8 million people in the 1950's, to what the New York Times reported as "home to 700,000 people, as well as to tens of thousands of abandoned buildings, vacant lots and unlit streets." (Davey and Walsh, 2013) Detroit changed from a thriving international city affectionately known as Motown for its music, culture, and automobile industries, to a city that filed for Chapter 9 bankruptcy, making it the largest municipal bankruptcy filing in U.S. history. Spiritual leaders have the responsibility to help those who have experienced multiple disorientations reflect on their personal relationships, socio-economic challenges, and loss of faith.

In June 2013, I attended a Word of Faith International Christian Center Convention in Southfield Michigan, just outside of Detroit. Word of Faith is a thriving ministry under the leadership of Bishop Keith A. Butler. I learned from Bishop Butler, Dr. Bill Winston, Reverend Kenneth Copeland, and other pastors. Between sessions, and in the evenings, I saw first-hand what happened to people who lost their jobs and were told that their job skills were no longer needed.

I am talking about ordinary, middle class, middle-age people whose jobs disappeared, and they were left to reflect on multiple Disorientations in their lives. When people were laid off, how many woke up in the morning, scrutinized their assumptions, values, and norms before making the decision to change their lives? How many of them searched for jobs and found that their job skills were no longer relevant for jobs in a changing, global economy?

Literally thousands of unemployed residents searched the want ads for work, only to find far more job seekers than jobs available. How many of those job seekers had to be retrained for the jobs that were listed? How many doubted their ability to learn new skills? More importantly, how many listened to the voice of the enemy, experienced anxiety, lost hope, and sought help for clinical depression?

Your efforts must enable people to question their own belief systems, cultural norms, and values. After speaking with you, they should be empowered to challenge their assumptions about long-standing relationships, and explore strategies for developing new patterns of behavior. Old habits must be discarded, so they can see life from a new and changed perspective.

THE THIRD KEY:
PERSPECTIVE TRANSFORMATION

Perspective Transformation is one of the more complex spiritual Keys needed to understand Spiritual Transformation. As we can infer from our own experiences, it is difficult to change our own perspectives or understanding of the reality we see and experience every day.

After our minds have undergone the first two Keys, Disorientation and Critical Reflection, we will have developed a more critical understanding and appreciation of how our social relationships and culture have shaped our beliefs, feelings and view of ourselves. Perspective Transformation requires us to take un-equal power in relationships into account, and help people develop an empowered sense of self. This changed understanding of self is the gateway through which Spiritual Transformation can take root and grow.

Evidence of Perspective Transformation is having new knowledge of self after you have undergone the process of breaking down mental barriers that constrained your ability to see yourselves in a new light. Understanding this process is essential to your ability to develop more functional strategies and resources for taking action. As such, it is critically important that you gain a clear understanding of this spiritual Key.

As pastors, teachers, and ministers, sometimes you might mistakenly interpret a persons' going through a conversion experience as a perspective transformation; however, they are not the same thing. When a person accepts Jesus Christ into their life, he or she may experience a feeling of euphoria, which is more appropriately associated with a Disorientation of the mind. However, sometimes feelings of euphoria are fleeting and do not help us understand the changes taking place in one's mind during the Perspective Transformation stage of learning.

To illustrate the complexity of this Key, I am reminded of a teaching that Dr. Bill Winston gave at the Word of Faith International Christian Center in June 2013. He described an experiment where a researcher put a predator fish and a gold fish in the same fish tank. It didn't take long before the predator fish got hungry and ate the gold fish.

As a means to change the reality of an un-equal power relationship between the fish, the researcher placed a see-through barrier in the tank that allowed the predator fish to see the gold fish swimming around, but blocked its ability to physically touch or eat the other fish. After a period of time, the researcher removed the barrier, and found that the predator fish swam right past the gold fish, and didn't eat it.

The predator fish learned that a barrier it could not see protected the other fish. But something else happened in that tank as well. The gold fish develop an empowered sense of self and swam right past the predator fish because it believed the un-equal power relationship changed and protected it.

To better understand what changed in the behavior of both fish, we can look at what happened in the tank using the Perspective Transformation Key. Perspective Transformation allows us to see that the transparent barrier altered the perspective of the un-even power relationship between the two types of fish, and caused them to change their perspectives of their realities. After the barrier was removed, a change in the behavior of both fish was apparent; however, physically, nothing prevented the predator fish from eating the gold fish.

Odd as it may seem, that same concept applies to people. Some people have learned over time to accept barriers to their progress, even after those barriers have been removed. As pastors, teachers, and ministers, we have to teach people that we "see" our reality through our eyes, not with them. After we better understand that concept, we can help people go anywhere their minds will take them. Until people learn they are free to pursue alternative courses of action, and that punishment for taking affirmative steps to reach their desired goals may have been substantially reduced or even eliminated, they may choose not to pursue any action they believe might lead to unpleasant consequences.

Now that you know Perspective Transformation results in an empowered sense of self, you are in a better position to understand that you may experience resistance if you try to help people see themselves from a new perspective, without their understanding that an un-equal power relationship may have changed. Keep in mind that our jobs as leaders, is to help people develop more functional strategies and resources for taking action. Without this new knowledge, you may experience the same frustration that other leaders have experienced when they tried to help people free themselves from mental barriers that constrained their abilities to act.

As leaders, we have to remind ourselves, as well as those we teach and minister to, what Hebrews 11:1 teaches us: *"Now faith is the substance of things hoped for, the evidence of things not seen."* Sometimes, we have to use knowledge and scripture to encourage people to accept the fact that they don't have to be able to see the power that is already in place to protect them.

To enable people to see themselves from new perspectives, you have to help them transform their minds and empower them to step out on nothing more than their faith in God to bring about changes they desire. If they do not develop an empowered sense of self and change their perspectives, they will be susceptible to powers of the enemy. Enemies of God deceive the eyes and blind the minds of believers of the word of God. New perspectives must be created that reveal alternative ways of knowing, and take un-equal power in relationships into account.

THE FOURTH KEY: SOCIAL ACTION

How many times have you taken action, only to realize that you leaped before you looked? I'm sure all of us can recall a time or two (ok, dozens for those of us who are keeping it real) when we rushed to judgment or otherwise made decisions and took action in haste that we later regretted. We can reduce those regrettable moments if we reflect critically on our prior learning, develop an empowered sense of self, and develop new perspectives of what is possible.

The Fourth Key, Social Action, is predicated on a deeper understanding of the conditions of one's changed reality or life circumstances, and considering the cost before taking action. Social Action assumes the existence of three fundamental attributes: people have the power to construct their own social and political realities; their racial/ethnic/cultural values and beliefs must be taken into consideration; and action taken generally serves the interests of dominant groups in society. It is this third attribute of Social Action that generates the most discussion because sometimes, ones racial/cultural identity may cause them to pursue a course of action not generally supported by the dominant culture.

When you help people think through which action to take, you must first consider the un-even power relationship between people who perceive they are unable to free themselves from the trappings of society, and those who may hold sway over them including spouses, employers, governmental agencies or other entities. Many people have been conditioned over time by educational institutions, their actual experiences, and through the projected reality presented by the media of the dominant culture where they live, to see themselves as unable to change their situations.

It is important to understand that people's cultural and racial identities have a powerful influence over how they see themselves. Your efforts must motivate people to act, because action is an essential part of Spiritual Transformation. You have to teach people that transformational change is a process that includes their having considered the costs and taking affirmative steps towards their new goals. Those steps may include enrolling in adult literacy programs, going back to college, or attending church services on a regular basis. Others may need to relocate if you learn that their current living situation will be detrimental to their family, economic security, or personal health and wellbeing.

Without Social Action, the scripture of James 2:26 makes it plain, *"For as the body without the spirit is dead, so faith without works is dead also."* If you recall the example of the expecting father who experienced multiple Disorientations after learning that his wife was about to give birth to their first child, you notice that he didn't take any action to resolve the speeding ticket he received, or help his boss get the presentation off his computer.

As his spiritual advisor, what would your advice to him be if he called you at home, right in the middle of a slightly warm discussion with your spouse about troubles in your marriage? And what if the slightly warm discussion was about how to stem the decline in membership in your congregation because they perceive you are not accessible when they called you for advice in times of need?

Using the principles of the Social Action Key as a guide, you first have to understand how to successfully navigate social action with your spouse, before you can help the expecting father. In the matter of a minute or two, while the tithing member of your congregation is waiting impatiently on hold, you have to convince your spouse to give you a minute to do God's work. A caring spouse or helpmeet would submit without consequences.

In your own marriage, you have to be able to determine if there is an un-even power relationship between you and your spouse and who holds the sway over whom in the marriage. Bear in mind that you and your spouse have the power to construct your own social reality. Your delaying the slightly warm discussion, if only for a brief moment, will better enable you to meet your spouse's needs.

When you get back on the phone with the panicked and soon to be father, you will only have a brief moment to hear him, help him gain a deeper understanding of the dilemmas he finds himself in, and make sure that he considers the costs of his actions. It is important to keep in mind that enemies of God are liars, and may try whispering in the expected father's mind things like "the cop is a racist. He only pulled you over because you're black." Or, "don't call the pastor, he wont help. You need to leave that church like everyone else."

You should be able to help him realize that he can get off the phone with you and text the password for his computer, along with the name of the presentation file, to his assistant. His assistant can get the presentation to his boss.

Further still, you can advise him that he can opt to fight the ticket at a later time. Some courts consider the birth of a child as a reasonable justification for speeding. Or, you can advise him to just pay it. The good news is that either option could be done at a later date. Taking these steps should enable you to change the perception that you are not available to help members of your congregation when they need you. You can then get off the phone so that you can give proper attention to your spouse and resolve your own issues.

The Social Action Key teaches us that people have the power to construct their own social and political realities, and that their cultural ethnic/racial values and beliefs must be taken into consideration. The enemy knows this, and will use it to convince people to make unhealthy choices.

As spiritual leaders, you have to reassure the father that you were there for him, and make it clear he got pulled over because of his actions (he was speeding), not because the cop was a racist. Understanding the essential elements of the Social Action Key will enable you to appreciate the conditions of your own reality or life circumstances, so you can teach others to consider the cost before taking action.

THE FIFTH KEY:
SPIRITUALITY

People from all walks of life have expressed a desire to enjoy the simple pleasures of life by gaining a deeper understanding of spirituality, and living in a way that honors God. The fifth Key, Spirituality, provides that clarity. After you have changed your perspective, and constructed new social and political realities, you honor God through your efforts to live by faith, not by sight. Roman's 12:3 teaches us, *"… God hath dealt to every man the measure of faith."* All people were born with "the" measure of faith. You have to identify the strength of your faith in God, and stand on it, to live abundant and prosperous lives.

The fifth Key, Spirituality, challenges you to develop a spiritual connection with God, stand on your faith in the grace of God, and accept changes in your life circumstances. Actions you take to honor God will cause changes to occur in the spirit of your mind. After which, the Holy Spirit will be empowered to use your spirit-led actions to build the Kingdom of God right here on Earth, in God's timing, not your own.

In recent years, we have seen numerous events that have challenged our perception of what is possible, and at the same time, brought our spiritual connection to God to the forefront. To illustrate this point, I introduce and briefly discuss four historically significant events that I believe impacted our spirituality, and faith in God. The first event was the 1995 Million-Man March on Washington, followed by the legacy of Dr. Martin Luther King Jr., the election of President Barack Obama in 2008, and finally the disgracing sex abuse allegations concerning nearly 3,000 Roman Catholic Priests.

On October 16, 1995, the world watched as 1.8 – 2 million African American men marched on Washington, D.C. in the spirit of Atonement, Reconciliation, and Personal Responsibility. (Boston University for Remote Sensing, October 27, 1997) I was among them, and bore witness to the largest, peaceful demonstration on the Capitol Grounds in the history of the United States.

Atonement, in the biblical sense, represents Jesus' suffering and death in redeeming mankind, and bringing about the reconciliation of God to man. Almost 2 million men Atoned for wrongdoing we caused our families, and the women who love us. We also proclaimed our faith in God before the world.

The second historical event was the 50th Anniversary of the Reverend Martin Luther King, Jr.-led demonstration for freedom and civil right for all Americans. In 2013, Americans and people from around the world celebrated the life of the slain civil rights leader. I also attended that important gathering.

The King event was special because Americans finally have a historical monument on the Capitol Grounds in Washington, D.C. that honors an African American, Dr. Martin Luther King, Jr. It was reported that tens of thousands of people gathered to commemorate and reflect upon Dr. King's message of non-violence, and the causes he gave his life to advance.

Fittingly, the third historically significant event that impacted our spirituality and faith in God was the election of Illinois Senator, Barack Obama as the 44th President of the United States of America on November 4, 2008. President Obama dedicated the Martin Luther King, Jr. Memorial on October 16, 2011. That was a memorable moment for President Obama, as he stood in front of the world as a shining example of the glory and power of God. I was fortunate to have been in Washington, D.C. for that event as well.

Most Americans failed to realize the significance of the date of President Obama's historic dedication of the King memorial. He chose October 16, or the 18th anniversary of the Million-Man March. We, the African American men who organized and participated in the March, proclaimed October 16, as Atonement Day.

Dr. Benjamin Chavis and David Caruth
at March Planning Meeting

That is the day African American men proclaimed as the Holiday we gave ourselves to honor God.

On his journey to becoming the first African American Commander in Chief, President Obama was subjected to ridicule from members of the media because his name reflects his father's African Muslim heritage. Somehow, his name, Barack Hussein Obama, became the basis for his religious beliefs, and he was labeled a Muslim.

His middle name, Hussein is Arabic in origin; however, his first name, Barack is Swahili, and his surname, Obama, is from the Luo tribe in Kenya. President Obama summarily dismissed their attacks on his Christian faith, and the media shifted its attention to his Pastor, Jeremiah Wright of Trinity United Church of Christ in Chicago. The media reported that Pastor Wright had given sermons to his congregation that members of the dominant culture found to be controversial.

At his inaugural address on January 20, 2009, after defeating Arizona Senator John McCain in the 2008 election, President Obama acknowledged the sacrifices of "our ancestors." It was not lost on us, as Americans, that a person of African heritage could be elected leader of the free world, and rule from the comfortable confines of the White House. He went on to reaffirm his Christian faith by mentioning "our enduring spirit," our "God-given promise," and the fact that we are "free" to pursue a "full measure of happiness."

While people from around the world welcomed President Obama's racial/cultural identity and his ascension to power, in America he was forced to defend his religious faith. Ultimately, he used his own racial/cultural identity to declare his faith in God, and to place Pastor Wright's comments in a social/historical context. To his credit, President Obama refused to disown Pastor Wright as a person; however, he distanced himself from some of Dr. Wright's teachings, and resigned his membership in the Chicago church.

The fourth, and most disturbing of the historical events that brought our spiritual connection to God to the forefront from 2001-2014, involved the Roman Catholic Church. This disturbing series of events has been widely reported around the world as the Catholic Church Sex Abuse Cases. Those allegations, investigations, and trials resulted in public ridicule and convictions of Catholic Priests for child sexual abuse crimes.

The crimes and lawsuits against the church's dioceses shook the core of nearly 1.6 billion Catholics around the world. Sadly, the court cases revealed that some leaders of the Catholic Church deliberately hid abusive behaviors of several of their Priests. Instead of disciplining the perpetrators, some leaders in the church moved them to other parishes where some of them continued their abusive behaviors.

As pastors, teachers, and ministers, we have to bear the burden of those revelations about the Catholic Church. Those events caused millions of people around the world to experience unpleasant Disorientations, go through the Critical Reflection process without the benefit of consulting their spiritual advisors, and caused many to dredge up memories of similar events in their own lives.

How many people underwent Perspective Transformations based on new knowledge of the Church, considered the costs, and took Social Actions to protect themselves from the Church? Your charge, as men and women of God, is to make sure that you understand all 6 dimensions of Spiritual Transformation before you use it to help people transform their thinking and change their lives. As members of one body of Christ, we have to help people restore their faith in God, the Holy Scripture, and in the power of the Holy Spirit.

We can no longer stand by and allow the media to dishonor the spiritual benefits of nearly 2 million African American men who honored God, because the idea of the March came through the Nation of Islam leader, Minister Louis Farrakhan. Keep in mind that Dr. King was a man of God, who many people despised and ridiculed, before he was murdered for taking action not supported by members of the dominant culture. President Obama was vilified for seeking to end two unpopular wars, and for his efforts to provide affordable health care benefits for all Americans. Finally, we have to use the power of the word of God to minister to millions of Catholics who felt betrayed by their priests and other leaders in their church.

As spiritual leaders, you have to demonstrate through your actions, not merely your words that you will take steps necessary to protect people, especially widows, children, the poor and vulnerable adults who come to you for help. People are spiritual beings and we have to help strengthen their faith and spiritual connection to God.

THE 6TH KEY:
CHANGE IN WORLDVIEW

The 6th and final Key of Spiritual Transformation, Change in Worldview, is the actual manifestation of knowing that you no longer see the world from the same perspective. If you grasped the knowledge presented in the previous 5 Keys, and internalized the essence of the information and teachings that were presented, than you received knowledge essential to helping people transform their lives.

Change in Worldview, is a process that enables people to see themselves from a new and empowered sense of self, and to have that worldview valued by the dominant culture. This new sense of self is built on our faith in the grace of God, and the understanding that people view the world through their own cultural/racial lens. What is true in one culture may not be true in another culture. Thus, people need to have their experiences understood from their own cultural/racial perspectives.

When people's worldviews change, they no longer see themselves from the same "old" worldview that they held prior to going through Spiritual Transformation. They can appreciate the uniqueness of diverse cultural identities, and the value of multiple worldviews. Think back to a time when you experienced a significant disorientation in your life. The occurrence of that event must have changed your view or perspective of reality, and resulted in you never being able to see the world that way again.

I remember when I was the Coordinator of Undergraduate Advisement at the University of Wyoming. I was introduced to a woman who was hired to oversee the Multi-cultural Affairs office in the College of Education. She held a Ph.D. and had vast amounts of international experience.

When we met, it was clear how proud she was of her South African heritage. To impress us, gain our respect, or acceptance, I haven't been able to determine which, she let us "minorities" know that back in South Africa, she was the equivalent of a Governor. I am certain she didn't intend to insult us by drawing attention to her positions of authority, or by the arrogance we perceived as she spoke about her accomplishments, but that is what happened.

In spite of how comfortable she felt addressing the educational needs of African American students, she didn't realize many of us fought to force our government and private businesses to divest American dollars from South Africa. We also fought to force her homeland to free Nelson Mandela, and to bring down the Apartheid form of government that enabled her to achieve the higher social status she enjoyed.

As a means to "cope" with the disorientation many of us experienced as a result of our conversation with our new colleague, some of us "minorities" gathered in my office and openly expressed how disgusted we were that the University hired her for such an important position. We considered my office a "safe zone" where people could gather to discuss issues from the perspective of one's own cultural/racial identity.

We debated among ourselves if we should "educate" our learned colleague about the differences between her worldview and ours. Further still, should we inform her about the social action we took to force her government to partially liberate millions of people of color in her homeland?

If the university's new "Minority Affairs" professor had taken the time to acquaint herself with our cultural/racial identities, perhaps she could have recognized that we saw ourselves from a new and empowered sense of self. To be sure, it was our presence at the university that resulted in her being hired, and not the other way around.

It was not lost on us that South Africa had far more people of color than Whites; however, Whites controlled the government and most other forms of worldly power. From our worldviews, it appeared to us South Africa needed all of its "White" residents to serve in positions of authority, regardless of their intellectual prowess or other capabilities, to control a country that size, and all of its "colored inhabitants."

In the end, South African President Nelson Mandela stood on his faith in God, and used the power of forgiveness to overcome centuries of hatred in South Africa. On December 5, 2013, leaders from around the world, including President Obama, and Retired South African Archbishop and Nobel Laureate Desmond Tutu, gathered to mourn his passing.

As a people, our Worldview's changed. The memorial to Dr. Martin Luther King stands as the only monument commemorating the life of an African American on the Capitol Grounds in Washington, DC. The King memorial is evidence that the dominant culture values our perspectives.

THE MARTIN LUTHER KING JR. MEMORIAL

CHAPTER FOUR

UNLOCKING THE LAW OF SPIRITUAL TRANSFORMATION

"And be renewed in the spirit of your mind."
Ephesians 4:23

Some of you may be wondering why I chose a pyramid with a keyhole at the top to illustrate the Law of Spiritual Transformation. The keyhole symbolizes the need to use spiritual keys of understanding to unlock the knowledge enclosed within. I wanted to make it plain that knowledge behind the 6 Keys of Spiritual Transformation would empower you to transform your thinking, and renew your mind.

I used the image of the pyramid for three reasons. First, I wanted to show a visual image of the three dimensions of The Law of Spiritual Transformation. The illustration allows visual learners to see all three dimensions of Romans 12:2. We have to move beyond deficit models of learning that reward individuals who excel under auditory theories of learning, and include ways to teach those with diverse learning styles.

Second, I wanted to recognize and honor ancient African civilizations. People of African heritage have no cause to see our history as inferior to the history of any other civilization or culture on earth. Even the ancient Greeks considered African/Egyptian pyramids as one of the 7 wonders of the world.

Third and most importantly, people everywhere in the world need to understand that African Americans embrace our connection to Africa. I freely acknowledge that victors of war write the history and that ancient African centers of learning, like Timbuktu and the Library of Alexandria, were destroyed. Nonetheless, Africa remains the cradle of all civilization, and African American people claim our birthright as sons of God who have always been present on the world stage.

Authors of the Torah, Quran, and the Holy Bible all acknowledge Ethiopia as a prominent African civilization. Holy Scripture teaches us in 1 Kings 10:13, *"And king Solomon gave unto the queen of Sheba all her desire, whatsoever she asked, beside that which Solomon gave her of his royal bounty. So she turned and went to her own country, she and her servants."* According to the Ethiopian Royal Chronicle, Queen Sheba returned to Ethiopia with the Ark of the Covenant, and the original 10 Commandments Moses received from God on Mount Sinai. (Raffaele, P. 2007) Ethiopians claim possession of the Ark to this very day.

The three dimensions of The Law of Spiritual Transformation are presented in the same order they appear in the Holy Scripture. The top layer is "be not conformed to this world." Which is followed by, "be ye transformed by the renewing of your mind." And the foundation level is to "prove what is that good, and acceptable, and perfect will of God."

The Law of Spiritual Transformation Illustration

In the book of Habakkuk 2:2, the Lord said, *"... Write the vision, and make it plain upon tables that he may run that readeth it."* Use the 6 Keys of Spiritual Transformation to unlock The Law of Spiritual Transformation and help people renew the spirit of their minds.

To unlock the Law of Spiritual Transformation, a person must first understand how to "be not conformed to this world." As you have learned, once a person experiences a Disorientation of the mind, they are ready to receive new learning. However, as spiritual leaders, you are not alone when you use your spiritual gifts to help people resist the temptation of conforming to the world. Enemies of God, and people who act as counsel of the ungodly, will compete with you to sway people's behavior. They will take the very same teachable moment during periods of Disorientation to sow seeds of doubt, mistrust, and confusion into the minds of believers.

People that assume the role as counsel of the ungodly usually know the person whose mind is in a state of Disorientation. However, they often lack compassion and encourage believers to focus their attention on financial or other worldly matters, rather than nurturing a spirit of brotherly love. You may have to shed light on tricks of the enemy, before you speak new knowledge into a person's life. Your efforts must help people go through the Critical Reflection process and scrutinize their assumptions, values, and norms to determine whether the information and/or knowledge learned in the past is useful for making forward-looking decisions.

Once they have scrutinized their assumptions, and understand their own salvation depends on their ability to receive scripture-based teachings, they are ready to transform their perspectives. Perspective Transformation enables them to undergo the process of breaking down mental barriers that once constrained their ability to act. It will result in a new empowered sense of self that empowers people to pursue courses of action that may not be supported by the dominant culture. It is at the Social Action stage of Spiritual Transformation where people can "be not conformed to this world." Thus, the top layer of the pyramid is unlocked.

The second dimension of The Law of Spiritual Transformation is to "be ye transformed by the renewing of your mind." The fifth Key, Spirituality, requires people to stand on their faith in the Grace of God to comprehend, receive, and embrace changed conditions in their lives. You must help believers mentally prepare their minds to receive instruction from the word of God, and to be led by the Holy Spirit. People can experience an abundant life, with a new empowered sense of self, because we already have "the" measure of faith, and we already "inherited" free and unmerited favor from God. Thus, the second tier of the pyramid is unlocked.

The foundation of The Law of Spiritual Transformation is to "prove what is that good, and acceptable, and perfect will of God." The 6th Key, Change in Worldview, together with the other 5 Keys, allows people to change their worldviews because they embraced the idea that people have diverse cultural/racial identities, and they considered the cost of un-equal power relationships before taking action.

The ruling elite in America did not support the 1995 Million-Man March on Washington. Those who marched, developed an empowered sense of self, stood on our faith in God, and pursued a course of action that was not generally supported by the dominant culture. Nearly 2 million African American men Atoning for our past behavior on the Capitol Grounds of the most powerful country in the world demonstrated our ability to go beyond fallible worldly influences and logic, and act according to the infallible logic of the perfect will of God. Thus the foundation of the pyramid is unlocked.

CONCLUSION

ACCEPT YOUR CALLING

"And we know that all things work together for good to them that love God, to them who are the called according to his purpose." Romans 8:28

The 6 Keys of Spiritual Transformation will help you transform the minds of people who may not have been born into families where wealth, possessions, tradition, and other forms of comfort are passed down from generation to generation. Speaking for myself and other people I was blessed to know as a child, and many I met later in life as adults, our spiritual journeys were less comforting. Our journeys included overcoming poverty, racial prejudice, learning disabilities and other challenges. We were exposed to crime, drugs, death, and multiple kinds of abuse. Some of us struggled to find food and shelter, and we sought out people who we hoped would protect us from physical violence, emotional cruelty, and sexual abuse.

Regardless of the condition of my birth, I was blessed. As a child, my mother read the Holy Scripture to me and taught me about the love of Jesus Christ. She also prayed over my life and spoke into it with the knowledge that a child's mind is fertile ground for learning. I recall her telling me that all things were possible through Christ, and I could achieve anything I set my mind to. I am grateful for the Holy Scripture and positive messages of hope she deposited in my mind.

As I matured into adulthood, I found the scripture my mom stood on to feed her children, even when there was no food in her kitchen. Hebrews 11:1 teaches us: *"Now faith is the substance of things hoped for, the evidence of things not seen."* My mom had faith in the grace of God, and she passed that knowledge along to me and my sisters and brothers.

In addition to biblical studies with my family, and learning from Apostles, Bishops, Pastors, and Ministers, I was blessed to earn advanced degrees in higher education. I learned from academic scholars who specialized in African American History, American Government and Politics, Public Administration, Adult Learning and Technology, and multiple theories of intelligence.

To bring forth this advanced level of understanding, I used my academic training, biblical studies, experiential knowledge, and spiritual gifts. I drew from my spiritual gifts of Teaching, Knowledge and Wisdom, to help you move beyond your natural ability to teach. However, with all the learning bought forth in this book, none is more important than the Holy Scripture. Proverbs 4:7 teaches us, *"Wisdom is the principal thing; therefore get wisdom; and with all thy getting get understanding."*

To bring about the change people seek, you must increase your understanding of scripture-based Spiritual Transformation. Supplement auditory preaching techniques with multiple theories of learning, and include multicultural/multiracial perspectives. Visual-learners learn best by seeing information, and Kinesthetic-learners learn best when movement is included in the learning environment.

In my spiritual journey as a Teacher, I would be remiss if I failed to call your attention to Revelations 13:9 *"If any man have an ear, let him hear."* Use the 6 Keys of Spiritual Transformation to teach people in search of transforming their lives how to look through a new lens that will bring into sharp focus alternative ways to create new worldviews of what is possible.

By gaining and applying the wisdom presented in this book, you can help people transform the psycho-cultural assumptions that distort the way they see themselves, and help them renew their minds. It is not enough to tell people that changing their thoughts from negative to positive will change their actions. Your efforts must carefully guide them through the 6 Keys of Spiritual Transformation, and empower them to stand on the Word of God to transform their lives.

When you look back on your service to God, let us pray the people you encountered were restored or made whole. Let there be evidence of your having served people in all of their diversity, and the least among us were not forgotten and left behind. Let there be a record of how you used the knowledge and wisdom gained over the years, to transform the minds of those who were unable to move past trials and tribulations on their own. In your final hours, let the people who know you say you used your gifts to help widows and the poor renew their minds, and enter the Kingdom of God. My prayer is that Spiritual Transformation will flow like God's precious, life giving water, from our Sheppard's of the Living Word. Let those who received the teaching and learning presented in this little book say, Amen.

ABOUT THE AUTHOR

Dr. David Caruth, founder and President of God's Perfect Timing Ministries, is a man of God and author of the book, God's Perfect Timing: Breaking the Cycle of Poverty with Education and Faith. He is a Teacher, in the Biblical sense, with more than 20 years experience helping people transform their lives.

Prior to moving to Washington DC to help provide education for the poor and under privileged residents of the District of Columbia, Dr. Caruth served as the Executive Director and owner of the National Center for Professional Development Solutions, in Denver Colorado, where he oversaw Center operations, hired and supervised faculty and staff, and gained higher education accreditation for all academic courses. He developed and taught graduate level courses in Transformative Learning Theory, Instructional Technology, Diversity & Motivation, Grant Writing, Portfolio Development and Personalized Learning Plans for practicing teachers and educators.

He also has expertise as a college professor having taught at Regis University, Lesley University, both at the graduate levels. As well as undergraduate teaching experience at the University of Wyoming, and The Metropolitan State College of Denver where he served as a fulltime African American Studies Professor.

As President of the Caruth-O'Leary Research Institute, he worked to eliminate drug use and gang violence in and around Section 8 housing complexes. Dr. Caruth holds a Ph.D. in Adult Learning & Technology, is an inspirational speaker, conference presenter, coach, mentor, husband and father.

Minister Debra and Dr. David Caruth

ABOUT GOD'S PERFECT TIMING MINISTRIES

GPT Ministries is a life long journey of spiritual faith that bridges the gap between active spirituality, God's people, and faith that miracles in our lives happen according to God's timing, not our own. We are a penetrating ministry rooted in the Holy Bible and the Word of God. We provide Transformational Leadership Training, Health & Healing Consulting, and address the needs of the poor using 5 areas of ministry that we believe are inspired by God to help break the often debilitating and crippling affects of poverty.

Transformational Leadership Training

Dr. Caruth is recognized internationally as a Transformational Learning scholar and Teacher. Our training combines empirical research and scripture-based teaching for national and international organizations, ministerial leaders, and others that desire to receive knowledge on how to use the transformational power of God to help people break free from the often debilitating affects of poverty and other afflictions.

Health and Healing Consulting

Minister Debra Caruth, Director of Ministries, is a licensed and ordained Minister of the Gospel of Jesus Christ and a Masters prepared Family Psychiatric/Mental Health Advanced Practice Nurse. We consult with national and international organizations, faith communities, and individuals to create custom health and wellness programs unique to the ideals, worldviews, and spiritual beliefs of the people being served.

Women's Ministry

Our Women's Ministry provides women with the tools necessary to address issues and concerns that affect their ability to overcome difficult challenges including pregnancy, abuse, trust, abandonment, and relationships with their children, mates, friends and other support groups.

Rite of Passage Ministry

The Rite of Passage Ministry provides males with spiritual guidance and knowledge of what is necessary to transition into manhood and become heads of households, mentors, husbands, fathers, and men of God.

Health and Healing Ministry

Our Health and Healing Ministry addresses both the natural symptoms of sickness and disease with community outreach, prayer and spiritual faith that illuminates the power of God and His divine presence to heal sickness, disability and disease.

Education Ministry

The Education Ministry addresses aspects of educational challenges stemming from early childhood education, special education, adult and continuing education, through college to bring about transformational change.

Faith Ministry

Our Faith Ministry utilizes the power of discernment and other spiritual gifts to help reveal everyday miracles that occur in our lives and increases our faith in the glory and power of God.

Contact us at:
God's Perfect Timing Ministries
P.O. Box 70080
Washington, DC 20024
www.gptministries.com

EXCERPT FROM:
GOD'S PERFECT TIMING

When I was 17 years old, my dad and I merely coexisted. He was working as a Maytag repairman and drove a light blue, 1970 Chrysler Newport. He could have abandoned my little sister Debora and me, but he didn't. His pride forced him to work and he did what he could to keep us from being homeless. We moved from one flee-bag motel in the red-light district of Colorado Springs to another until he managed to pay the rent on a three-bedroom apartment on the northern part of Nevada Avenue. Debbie and I were happy to have a place to live and we were glad that we could tell people where we lived instead of telling them we lived on North Nevada Avenue. The year was 1977 and I was just beginning my senior year of high school.

To get to school, most of the time I walked the five miles, to and from school. Our apartment complex was a huge, multi-family complex, just north of the city on Highway 85-87 from I-25. The complex was isolated and built to warehouse low-income renters who were just a notch above trailer park status. Walking along the street to get to school meant walking along North Nevada Avenue on gravel where truckers parked their rigs, ate fast food, or solicited prostitutes. There were no sidewalks, but the view of Pikes Peak was breathtakingly magnificent.

Sometimes, rather than walking along the street to school, I shortened the distance by walking through the wilderness and crossing Fountain Creek that ran alongside the highway. I crossed the creek by walking across a 12-inch pipe, 50 yards long and 20 feet above the crystal clear water. Other times, I walked across the creek that was often covered by thin ice during the winter months. Many times, the ice caved in under my weight and I fell in, but I kept going. I ignored the freezing cold waters and the pain I felt when my hands and feet went numb.

This particular day in August, my dad agreed to pick me up after football practice. I waited for him near the parking lot that was mostly vacant and dimly lit by light posts, but he never came. It was cool and dark outside and I knew the way home. To get home, I walked down Fillmore hill, crossed I-25 until I reached Nevada Avenue. While I was walking down Nevada Avenue past the K-Mart and red-light district motels, I flirted with the prostitutes who propositioned me. Somehow talking to the prostitutes changed my focus on the future to the here and now. In the here and now, I was hungry and broke and on top of that, I was exhausted from a week of practice and from working my part-time job as a dishwasher on the weekends.

As I continued along my way, I walked past the dog track where desperate gamblers tried to beat the odds. I saw my dad through the fence throwing down a handful of losing tickets. He had lots of company and somehow, he and the other losers appeared to be delighted by their misfortune and smiled broadly.

As far as I could tell, my dad gambled all of my life, and rarely won. When I got home, there was no food in the apartment and only ice and water in the fridge. I was hungry, angry with my dad, and I prayed to God that day. I challenged God to prove to me that He really existed.

God wasn't happy with the anger and challenge in my prayer, but He answered it anyway. The next week, I got struck by the largest bolt of lightning ever to hit a person who lived to tell about it. In the book of Job, Chapter 38, Verse 35, God asked: "Can you make lightning appear and cause it to strike as you direct?"

When the lightning struck, I was at practice on the football field at Coronado High School when a bolt of lightning ripped through the clear blue sky and found its mark on the very patch of dirt where I stood. My coaches later told me that the thunder that followed was so loud that it leveled all of the other players and coaches on the field at the time. What I know for sure is, that the lightning bolt that hit me was not an accident of nature, and that God didn't allow me to accept death.

The lightning bolt hit me in the head, cracked my football helmet, entered my body through the left frontal lobe of my brain, traveled down my body right past my genitals, down my legs, and exited through both ankles. I still have the scars to prove it.

My doctors used conventional wisdom to determine that my left-brain controlled hidden talents including memory, vision, language, spelling and reading, as well as doing algebra. They believed that each talent in the left-brain is a complex network of different processes, beyond those mentioned here, but injuries in that area of the brain often resulted in serious loss of those specific talents. In other words, my doctors believed that the quality of my life was going to be severely diminished.

As I lay dead on the ground, I accepted death. For a brief moment, my spirit left my body and joined the spiritual world. While in the spiritual world, time didn't exist, as we know it and I felt no pain. In death, understanding God's will didn't happen as we experience it on a daily basis, but through instant understanding that can only be described as taking less than a nanosecond.

In a split second, I saw my own life filled with struggle and pain. I saw misery, sorrow, loneliness and the pain that I would have to endure throughout my life. I also saw moments of unexpected joy, triumph over adversity, and happiness. I hoped against knowing, in vain, that I would not have to live that life, feel the pain of being hit by lightning, and have to live with the permanent injuries that resulted.

From the moment that I got struck by lightning, God's message to me was crystal-clear and unambiguous. He was not ending my time here on Earth; instead, He was letting me know that He heard my prayers and that He had the power to change my life forever.

Scripture and References

Boston University for Remote Sensing (October 27, 1997). http://www.bu.edu/remotesensing/research/completed/million-man-march/ABC- TV funded researchers at Boston University estimated the crowd size to be about 1,800,000 attendees, close to 2 million.

Caruth, D. (2011). God's Perfect Timing: Breaking the Cycle of Poverty with Education and Faith. Bloomington, IN: WestBow Press.

Caruth, D. (2000). African American Male Transformative Learning: An Afrocentric Study of the Million-Man March. (Doctoral dissertation, University of Wyoming, 2000)

1 Corinthians 1:5 "That in everything ye are enriched by him, in all utterance, and in all knowledge;"

1 Corinthians 12:1 "Now concerning spiritual gifts, brethren, I would not have you ignorant."

1 Corinthians 12:4, "There are diversities of gifts, but the same Spirit."

1 Corinthians 12:8-10, "For to one is given by the Spirit the word of wisdom; to another the word of knowledge by the same Spirit; to another working of miracles;

to another prophecy; to another discerning of spirits; to another divers kinds of tongues; to another the interpretation of tongues."

1 Corinthians 12:28-29, "And God hath set some in the church, first apostles, secondarily prophets, thirdly teachers, after that, miracles, then gifts of healing, helps, governments, diversities of tongues. Are all apostles? are all prophets? are all teachers? are all workers of miracles?"

Davey, Monica; Walsh, Mary Williams (July 18, 2013). "Billions in Debt, Detroit Tumbles Into Insolvency." The New York Times, July 19, 2013.

Ephesians 4:23 "And be renewed in the spirit of your mind."

Gardner, H (1993) Multiple Intelligences: The Theory in Practice. New York, NY: Basic Books.

Habakkuk 2:2 "And the LORD answered me, and said, Write the vision, and make it plain upon tables, that he may run that readeth it.

Hebrews 11:1 "Now faith is the substance of things hoped for, the evidence of things not seen."

Hosea 4:6 "My people are destroyed for lack of knowledge: because thou has rejected knowledge, I will also reject thee, that thou shalt be no priest to me: seeing thou has forgotten The Law of thy God, I will also forget thy children."

James 2:26 "For as the body with the spirit is dead, so faith without works is dead also."

Job 38:35, "Canst thou send lightnings, that they may go, and say unto thee, Here we are?"

1 Kings 10:13, "And king Solomon gave unto the queen of Sheba all her desire, whatsoever she asked, beside that which Solomon gave her of his royal bounty. So she turned and went to her own country, she and her servants."

Matthew 13:5-6 "Some fell upon stony places, where they had not much earth: and forthwith the sprung up, because they had no deepness of earth; And when the sun was up, they were scorched; and because they had not root, they withered away."

Mezirow, J. (1991) Transformative Dimensions of Adult Learning. San Francisco, CA: Jossey-Bass.

Proverbs 1:7 "The fear of the Lord is the beginning of knowledge: but fools despise wisdom and instruction."

Proverbs 4:7 "Wisdom is the principal thing; therefore get wisdom; and with all thy getting get understanding."

Proverbs 4:22 "For they are life unto those that find them, and health to all their flesh."

Proverbs 9:9 "Give instruction to a wise man, and he will be yet wiser: teach a just man, and he will increase in learning."

Raffaele, P. (2007, December), Keepers of the Lost Arc? Smithsonian Magazine. http://www.smithsonianmag.com/people-places/keepers-of-the-lost-ark-179998820/.

Revelations 13:9 "If any man have an ear, let him hear."

Romans 8:28 "And we know that all things work together for good to them that love God, to them how are the called according to his purpose."

Romans 12:2 "And be not conformed to this world: but be ye transformed by the renewing of your mind, that ye may prove what is that good, and acceptable, and perfect will of God."

Romans 12:3 "For I say, through the grace given unto me, to ever man that is among you, not to think of himself more highly than he ought to think; but to think soberly, according as God hath dealt to every man the measure of faith."

Romans 12: 6-7, "Having then gifts differing according to the grace that is given to us, whether prophecy, let us prophecy according to the proportion of faith; Or ministry, let us wait on ministering: or he that teacheth, on teaching."

Romans 12:8, "Or he that exhorteth, on exhortation; he that giveth, let him do it with simplicity; he that ruleth, with diligence; he that sheweth mercy, with cheerfulness."